the darkest hours

chloé marcellino

The Darkest Hours

Copyright © 2023 Chloe Marcellino

All Rights Reserved

IBSN: 9798862263886

The Darkest Hours

To my mother, who gave me everything even when there was nothing

The Darkest Hours

The Darkest Hours

contents

Acknowledgments……Pg 7

The Hurt…………...Pg 11

The Mourning………..Pg 83

The End…………....Pg 155

The Darkest Hours

The Darkest Hours

Acknowledgements

Who to start with but the one who gave me life: my mother. The women who taught me that love doesn't have to hurt and who loved me when all I wanted to do was fade away. I also wish to acknowledge the educators within my life, for without their wisdom and dedication to my successes, such a book would not be here. From studying poetry with both of my secondary school English

The Darkest Hours

teachers and watching them grade exam paper after exam paper, to present day me as a published author. I truly feel in debt to their dedication.

And to the others. The ones who stepped up. The friends who along the way have stood up for me and stood me up, on my own two feet again and reminded me to keep going, no matter how hard the days were. You reminded me how great life can be and I will never be able to repay you for that.

The Darkest Hours

Finally, to those who wish to

move on, I acknowledge

you. I see your pain and

I am with you every step of the way.

This book is for all of us

The Darkest Hours

The Darkest Hours

the hurt

The Darkest Hours

Tragedy

This tale is one of tragedy. the circumstances of blood.

dictated, and written by men.

The Darkest Hours

The Darkest Hours

Loving you
was like living in
the darkest hours

and now dawn is rising.

The Darkest Hours

The Reaper

I dug my grave when I was three.
that was the first time
you dared me to look death
in the eyes.

The Darkest Hours

A Child

I was a child, and you should have
known better.

I may have been pretty
I may have been bright
but I was just a girl,
how could that be
right?

at night I feel you looking at me
eyes that aren't even there, and I
pull down my imaginary skirt even
though I know you're not there.

you marked me
like I was your
territory.
stone cold fear burned into my skull.

but I'll never forget
that I was a child,
and that you should have known
better.

The Darkest Hours

Stronger

But it made you stronger, they said.
But I didn't need to be stronger.

I was a child.

The Darkest Hours

Life

you say life isn't fair.
try telling that to the seven-year-old
hiding behind the chair. defenceless
and shaking; the colour of grey. a six-
foot, aged man seeking its prey.

so, until your pristine toes
have walked a mile
in my tattered shoes,
don't you dare decide to deem
how life isn't fair to you.

The Darkest Hours

Tick, Tick, Boom

I think you liked it.
making me cry
and lie.
it made you tick.

I see your eyes twinkle
as my skin burns with scars.
does it give you satisfaction to know
someone would cling to you
forever.

you say you weren't like that,
and I suppose you weren't.

you were worse.

The Darkest Hours

Fair

how is it fair that you can
forget me
and carry on like I never happened.

and I can't.

The Darkest Hours

Pleasing

I live to please other people
because I don't know how
to please myself.

The Darkest Hours

The Stars

fathers and daughters shine
together like stars in
constellations of love.

I guess there were faults in our stars.

The Darkest Hours

Violations

eyes blackened and boundaries
crossed. tears on a bed, made for
single occupancy.

the handprints will fade but I will
always be marked by your enraged
violations

The Darkest Hours

Parental Responsibility

The day I started
having to beg for your love
should have been the day I left.

That was never
meant
to be my job

The Darkest Hours

Fatherhood

I think I will ask the universe
everyday
why you were my father?

The Darkest Hours

Drowning

I swallow your deeds,
choking on your words.
they are slowing
killing me.

consuming me
from the inside out.
a riptide of guilt.

I am drowning
to save you.
but the funny thing is
I know you
would never
do the same.

The Darkest Hours

Somewhere in the Orange

somewhere in the orange,
I lost you
on a warm summer night.
the night of the first bruise.

your voice turned into glass
shattered on the linoleum,
cut my heart into a million pieces
that you auctioned off
at noon

somewhere in the orange
on that warm summer night
I lost who I was.

The Darkest Hours

The Victim

hushed murmurs line
the streets of houses
I used to know
watchful eyes peering
over windowsill walls

in such a place
I will always walk
alone
and the truth
will never be spoken.

because until you can stop
playing the victim

I will always be the one to
blame.

The Darkest Hours

*The Monsters Who Haunted The
Underworld*

When was it the day,
that we finally met,
locked eye to eye

a random Tuesday
in mid november

or have you
just always been
here

like the monsters who
haunted the
underworld
of that bedroom.

The Darkest Hours

Absence

the absence
of bruises
is not the same as
the absence
of scars.

sometimes it's worse.

The Darkest Hours

The Cycles of Hurt

hurt people go on
to do the same.
over and over
like the turning of time
as their closest lovers become
enemies.

but that will never
make it ok.

to inflict the thing
that broke you,
on someone who
just wanted to love you.

The Darkest Hours

Lengths of Love

I wish that I had
never begged you
to love me.

in those moments
you saw what lengths I would go to,
the things I would say
in a failed effort
to make you stay.

and used it

to bring out
the worst in you
because I couldn't ever
stop wanting
to love you.

The Darkest Hours

Pain

The pain never
came from
your scars or
the bruises.

but from the fact
that you would apologise
and promise to change
and never did.

but every time I believed
you.

The Darkest Hours

Disobedience

I am not afraid
of the end

when it came down to it
I would rather die
than disobey him

let that sink in.

The Darkest Hours

The Fall

to fall,
a verb moving rapidly
and without control.
irregular.

I guess I am just
not the sort of person
somebody would
fall in love with.

it seems like people only
fall
out of love with me

or not even
love me at all.

The Darkest Hours

Light Years

When our eyes met
for the final time
we were light years away

not in proximity
but in souls
we were mere meters from
one another
no man-made measure
could name it so,
the universe did.

staring into cooling iris'
how gravity
could pull us this far
how suddenly being
your little girl
just was not enough anymore.

but it wasn't suddenly, was it

The Darkest Hours

and it was never gravity

you let me go
watched me float away
into a vast atlantic

we were light years away

but in truth
I could still
touch you

The Darkest Hours

Lessons Learned

It was a lesson
to be learnt.

beatings and belittling
for simply wanting you
to care

why

you weren't meant to be
the one who
taught me
how much love hurts

The Darkest Hours

Mother Courage

I haven't seen my father
for a while
crouching in front of his door
my presence is unaware.

my knuckles bang sonatas
along the oak.

I thought you deafened my
cries with your pillows
because
they were too hard to bear.

but the day
I plucked up the courage
to bang down that door
I realised you were
never there.

you left me
a long time

The Darkest Hours

before mother courage
arrived

The Darkest Hours

Behind Bottled Doors

Behind every
alcoholic father

is a scared little girl
begging him
to love her

and not the drink.

The Darkest Hours

Empty Bottles

it's unexplainable.

watching you shovel
drugs down
your throat for the disease
I apparently made up.

listening to unmet promises
as I empty recycling bins
fuelled by your
intoxication.

or your empty threats as
you open another
bottle.

helping you to the toilet
whilst I sit
in a cloth of my filth

The Darkest Hours

sopping wet rags
soaked with bleach
and tears
bin bags full of ashes:
the ghosts of
better days.

nothing quite prepares you
to look after a parent
when you can't even
look after yourself

The Darkest Hours

Bleeding Love

you stabbed me
in the back.

but still stood there
and wondered
why I was bleeding.

The Darkest Hours

Belief

you have
to believe in yourself.

there will be times in your life
where you are the only one
who does.

The Darkest Hours

Underestimate

Everything is
a show off when you
underestimate me
that much

The Darkest Hours

Asking For It

I was asking for it was I
I ask

your reply ached
with sexist confidence

and well
I must have been extraordinary
because
I was asking for it
long before I could
speak.

The Darkest Hours

Salt in The Wound

Salt and sugar,
are the same until
you pour onto
your open wounds

I learnt that the hard way.

The Darkest Hours

Black Holes

my heart carried the light of a
thousand splendid suns
and was drowned
completely
by one night in your darkness.

a black hole powered by
fantasied love.

The Darkest Hours

This Is Going To Hurt

my darling,
this is only just
the beginning

and I am afraid
it is going to hurt
for a very long time.

The Darkest Hours

Starvation

you piled my body
sky high with
materialism

greed and
intricate silk patterns
a pillar of capitalism.

to fill the void
burrowed by t
he most painful of
diseases

the starvation of love

The Darkest Hours

Death

I wanted to die
when I didn't even know
what it was like
to live

The Darkest Hours

Coat Hangers

If the coat hangers could speak,
they would rewrite fate.

their stories
and broken words
would take you down.

the one stained crimson
from a night with
your violence

the one burdened in black

to the one that was asking for it.

the tale at the end
of the rail
is lost for words
the deepest sorrow of all.

The Darkest Hours

the nappy
and the baby grow
who didn't know
how to say no.

The Darkest Hours

Crumbling Foundations

I watched
them fall

in love
out of love and down
the spiral staircase
of fate.

I was the product
their proof of existence
but as the earth
continued to spin

I became outdated
and the void began to part
once more.

sucking away
the facades of seeming
perfection.

and I was what was left.

The Darkest Hours

a final artifact for
the museums
to ponder

a mismatched puzzle
desperately trying not to
fall apart

on crumbling foundations

of love

The Darkest Hours

The Feast

I feast on fantasies
of places where
our love could have
flourished

a room with white curtains
and enough love for two

The Darkest Hours

My Immortal

Scared to leave
Nervous to love
and terrified to live

simple existence
was horrifying

The Darkest Hours

To Be Read

Life isn't like
what it is in
the books

you can't skip this chapter
or re-read the line

put it down,
discard it
when something better
comes along.

this isn't
some to be read list
this is real life

and it hurts.

The Darkest Hours

The Breaking of Hearts

The biggest heartbreak was that
I couldn't stop
loving you.

even when I knew
you never loved me.

The Darkest Hours

Mirrored Hearts

I saw our tragedies
mirrored in
broken hearts

battle scars
and antiseptic wipes; tears
flooding the valley
of things we used
to be.

it broke me
to see reflections of myself
in the scars
of others

The Darkest Hours

Google Searches

Google gave you
a hundred million results
for the question of
how to hit me
in ways hidden

to keep out the bloodhounds
from our situation
under the radar

but nothing when
I search

how to stop him killing me.

The Darkest Hours

The Probability

There was logic
amongst your evil
and within my madness.

I came back time and
time again
because you were all so
predictable.

methodical

fight
hit
forgive
repeat

over
and
over again.

every time worse than the last
but it was familiar

The Darkest Hours

I knew you would
do it

who is to say
that if I had moved on
the next man
wouldn't have
done the same

The Darkest Hours

Almost

We were the saddest story
to ever come out
of that town.

a victim of almost.

we almost made it

I was almost good enough for you

you almost loved me

The Darkest Hours

Too Late

You never once told me
that there would never
be love
but watched
in festering contentment
as my soul wasted away

and as I got older,
enough to understand
it was all
too late.

The Darkest Hours

Your Personas

daddy and father
are two different people

daddy hugged me
but father constricted

daddy smelt like summer
and an aftershave called
contentment
whilst father reeked
of alcoholism

and when daddy lifted me up
to place my star
on top of the Christmas tree

father couldn't get up off
of the sofa

too blacked out to see the stars
in my eyes slowly
stop twinkling.

The Darkest Hours

Memories Of The Future

It doesn't end well
does it?

the memories of a six-year-olds future

The Darkest Hours

Mother Tongue

my mother swallowed
her tongue
and I was born with it

and if she got out
so will I

The Darkest Hours

Choices

I chose to love you
when I didn't even know
what love was.

and you chose
not to love me
because you didn't know
what it was
either

The Darkest Hours

Plastics

I was your plastic,
and I was perfect.
moulded to standards
and status quos
man-made to be
beautiful

just the way you liked me

and then I was a plastic:
a pollutant,
disposable,
and what you saw
as the reason to blame
for your toxic masculinity.

my plastic perfection
was just too much for you
to resist.

and knees are so easy to
pry open.

The Darkest Hours

The Hiding

Mother hushed us.
our cries silenced
and hidden in broom closets

a sanctuary

it confused me why
we went
into hiding

until I realised
that it wasn't daddy
who was coming home
anymore

The Darkest Hours

Stab Wounds

Childhood was a knife
severed through
the heart.

you can disband the knife
and
discard my body

but we still bleed out

our wounds lay bare.

The Darkest Hours

All Too Well

It was a feeling known
all too well

of being everything
in beauty's grace that
the Gods themselves stand
to praise
like anti-heroes

and it still
not being enough
to satisfy the hunger
of his humanity

there glasses shattered
and so did
my heart

The Darkest Hours

Too Young

I cannot begin to understand
what it is that I did to
deserve
this

the burden of
so much pain
for someone so young

too young
for this

a child

The Darkest Hours

Spines

We were children
when the world came
crashing down

and I guess our spines
didn't have the backbone
to walk us away then

The Darkest Hours

Silent Creatures

Drowning is
a silent battle
suffered

and once the
sadness passes us by,
comes the waves

of anger
that I called for help times that
were countless
until I was hoarse
like agriculture

but no one came

saving myself from creatures,
demons sucking me slowly
from the pleasures
of being earth bound

The Darkest Hours

do you know
how much it hurt

pleading like a temptress for
somebody to notice me

I know that it wasn't
too late
but it could have been.

The Darkest Hours

One More Time

The courage to love
just one more time,

is what got me
into this mess.

The Darkest Hours

The Betrayals

The clock struck nine.
the last night that
you were mine.

a betrayal,
that I wasn't meant
to find

scattered our memories
on shattered glass
and broken picture frames

etched on hearts
like scars

and when you shout
your final bow
that it wasn't your fault

I cry

The Darkest Hours

because it wasn't
mine either

it was an abyss
white snow
that fell
a long, long time ago

but it isn't crazy
how our souls
turned into
strangers

and the ice became colder

The Darkest Hours

The Darkest Hours

The Darkest Hours

the mourning

The Darkest Hours

The Fruit Bowl of Sexism

I was an apple.
Sweet and rosy
till you dropped your burden.
the apple of your eye.
now I am blemished and bruised;
too bitter to be tasteful.

Now I am a banana,
And I stick out like a sore thumb.
People no longer seem to look at me,
the way they did when I was young.

Still as sweet
but now I am fruitful.
The object of society's eye.
Wanted and taunted,
Photographed and flaunted.

It's bittersweet
to be tossed to one side
when you show
signs of use

The Darkest Hours

Daddy's Issue

when I look in the mirror,
I see him.
staring straight back at me.
I am my father's daughter,
but I do not want to be.

a heat rises in my chest
my fists clench
when they should have been
held.

and then I see him
shamefully unwanted.
I no longer wish to be
his angry little girl
anymore.

All I wished for
was to be wanted.

The Darkest Hours

A Whole

a part of me died
the day I left.
I am not a whole being.
a delicate collection of fractures.

Behind me
is a creature,
one that shall never be named,
but dares to be.
and visits me in darkest nightmares
that won't go away.

the day I left,
a part of me died.

and now I am starting to
understand why.

The Darkest Hours

Locked Away

there is a little girl trapped
in the place I grew up.
banging on closed doors,
with pleas to be loved.

but the doors were locked
and nobody came.

now the walls are gone
and the windows are all smashed
but that little girl is still there.

her voice is fading:
a deafening silence.

no-one hears her scream.

The Darkest Hours

Lethal

your deadliest of traps
that kept me coming back to you
time after time
never escaped your hands
but from your lips

I love you.

The Darkest Hours

Heartache

I haven't heard your voices in years,
but my heart still remembers
all of the things you told me
I would never be.

The Darkest Hours

Free Trial

my children won't be
the fucked up free trial
you always made my life
out to be.

The Darkest Hours

Familiarity

nothing is safer than the scent
of familiarity.
maybe that's why
I think
of going back.

I wouldn't say it hurts less
to be beaten with
familiarity.

but I guess it grew
to be a comfort in a world
far less inviting.

The Darkest Hours

Poisons

I was a bee
and you were
a wasp.

my sting brewed
a cauldron coming to boil.
it would be the death
of me to use it.
so I never did.

your sting was potent and
mercurial.
overspilling with confidence
and vanity.

how is fair that we brew
poisons of the same vine,
and you can inflict with delight
the thing that will kill me
to display.

The Darkest Hours

Dining Tables

one table two chairs,
two mugs and
a pair of hands,
cradling tea
made for two.

the same as everyday
why weren't you there?

The Darkest Hours

Andromeda

in another world
maybe we would have made it.
watched each other grow
sipping coffee into
the dawn.

you'd go first
and I would follow.
the heartache.
six feet under
and inches apart.

maybe in Andromeda,
another galaxy
you could have loved me
like I loved you.

The Darkest Hours

Drunken Hypocrisy

You are my special little girl he'd say
but the abuse was mine
not my sister's.

I will always protect you he said
lifting me up to kiss
the shrivelled skin of the woman
who gave me these scars.

I love you he says through
his storms of rage.
the drunken hypocrisy
makes me laugh.

You said all the right things
to make me think
I could stay

but underneath your drunken facades
I know you could never
love me.

The Darkest Hours

Possessions

I lost who I was
trying to keep you.

and my moving on
doesn't erase the pain
the love we had caused

but it makes it
at least bearable
to think of.

The Darkest Hours

Maybe

maybe the reason why
I cannot love is because
all the love I have known hurts.

The Darkest Hours

The Ways I Hate You

I hate the ways
you made me feel.
worthless and numb inside.

the ways you made me feel
unlovable
your tactic to keep me
always close by.

I hate the way I keep forgiving you
I know you will do it again

you were never sorry

and I hate the ways
I still love you
even though
I do not want to.

The Darkest Hours

Love and Sex

I can only have sex
I cannot make love

because I do not know what love is.

The Darkest Hours

The Hole

I don't want to live
in a hole anymore
somewhere
my mother gave birth.

and died

trapped in an endless pit
of misery and despair.
with people
who say they care

I don't want to live
in a hole
anymore

The Darkest Hours

Pieces of Soul

you shattered my being
my soul is now no less than
a million pieces of
jigsaw puzzle.

scattered
to the four winds

and now I can't make a
home anywhere.

because all that is left are
the tattered pieces of heart that
you scattered
from your coat pocket as
you slammed my door
a final time.

The Darkest Hours

A Slave

the thing that hurt the most
were never the bruises
or the cruel intentions

but the fact that you never
wanted me.

or loved me

and yet you still watched me
spend eighteen years a slave
working for something that
you could never give.

The Darkest Hours

My Future

I do not hate you
but I am scared
of you

because you never truly left
and now
I can't either

and it's scary.

sincerely, my future

The Darkest Hours

Battle Scars

I have scars from battles
I should never have
had to fight.

The Darkest Hours

Unlearned

I had to unlearn it
all the hurting
the loving
the breaking
and
forgiving.

I gave it all up the day I
left,

but now as a
mother
do I have to learn it all back

you showed me that you cannot
love
two people at the same time
and I won't let her live
like that.

but I do not wish to go back
again

The Darkest Hours

I want to keep unlearning
all of those things you taught me
about love

The Darkest Hours

Nothing Heals

I hold onto the pain
because that is all I have left
of you.

it shouldn't be this way

you aren't dead
but it's even more
silent that it would
have been
if you were six feet
under

or scattered.

at least
your ghost would have
been of some comfort.

but now

The Darkest Hours

I have just the burden of
a broken heart
and that is a heavy price
to pay.

The Darkest Hours

Fairy Tales

mothers die and father's cry
that's what fairy tales
taught me.

that all good things come
to those who wait and
to have the courage to love when
all you can feel
is hate.

but love stings and
father's bruise
that's what life
has taught me.

my life was never
a fairy tale
it was a brothers Grimm tale
of reality.

The Darkest Hours

Waiting Rooms

I waited and
waited and
waited for you
to come.

but when that day
finally came
it was another person I was
running
to embrace.

The Darkest Hours

Behind Tears

behind the tears
and the lies

behind all of
the silence

is a little girl
waiting to tell
her story,

and begging
the others
to believe her

and not him

The Darkest Hours

Sliding Doors

in another universe
my mother turned right
instead of left
at the fork in the path

and I ended up
with a father who
actually loved me.

The Darkest Hours

Before Everything

I sometimes wonder
who I was before
my world collapsed
and love became
rare,
like gold dust

but there was no
before you.

this is my life.

The Darkest Hours

Bad Feminists

all I ever wanted was
a red door and
a bay window with
white curtains.

love I suppose

maybe I am just
a bad feminist.

The Darkest Hours

Uncharted Waters

I'm sailing a boat of uncertainty
through a mist of guilt and tragedy,
reminding myself that
even the grimmest of rivers
end up somewhere safe
at sea.

I do not know how to feel

the pain and the anger
it's all I have left of us,
and even though you hurt me,
I don't want to let it go.

your abuse
was a blanket of certainty
on an island infested
with the vultures of your past
and now I have nothing.

The Darkest Hours

I am navigating uncharted waters
and I have no idea
where to go
next.

The Darkest Hours

Broken Pieces

I know that you are
broken.

but I only have
enough glue
to mend one broken heart.

The Darkest Hours

Groundhog Day

it's like Groundhog Day
the loving
the fighting
the bruises
and then
the forgiving.

until one day
I looked at the clock
and realised that
eighteen years had passed.

The Darkest Hours

Someplace Better

I wished my soul
to another universe

a long
long time ago

the hope was that
one of us
would make it to the part
with a happy ending.

it split me in two
to let myself go

but I could carry on

knowing that a part of me
was some place where nothing
was wrong.

The Darkest Hours

One Way Ticket

you could have taken me
to the moon
and back

and instead booked
me
a one-way ticket to
hell.

somewhere
you should have been
instead.

The Darkest Hours

Forgiveness

As a child
I used to cry
I forgive you

it was easier
that way
the only way to survive

but now
with adulthood in front of us
and children
at my side

its
how could you

and that day
the child died.

The Darkest Hours

How To Live

the day it all began
I stopped *living*

piece by piece
organs shutdown
or
sold themselves off to
more deserving souls

and
when escape became
a necessity
not a luxury
I couldn't *breathe*

because I had forgotten
how to live.

The Darkest Hours

A Monster Called Reality

the scariest part is that
we are taught
to be scared by ogres
of the villains
in fairy tales
and the monsters
who lived under our beds.

but in reality
the only monster
was you.

The Darkest Hours

The Guilty

why do I feel guilty
for the crimes that you
committed?

The Darkest Hours

The Flood

Every time I walk the street
with a man
I go back to being
a nine-year-old girl

and terrified

it all comes flooding back.

the anger and
then the betrayal

hurt
and lies
the pouring of
the tears I cried,
in goblets made of gold

they all come
flooding back.

The Darkest Hours

The Deserving Ones

I gave my whole being
to you.

trusted you
and watched you
tear me to shreds,
a big bad wolf
with his grandma

and now
I have nothing
to give to the people
who are deserving of
my soul.

The Darkest Hours

Biological Dispositions

I wished so hard
not to be like you
but it was
my biological disposition

that you left
and mother stayed
and carried on,
with the burdens that
your cardboard boxes
couldn't fill.

and full circle
it is me
who is leaving you.

The Darkest Hours

Them And Us

There was never an us
just you and me

and in the end
you left me.

The Darkest Hours

Universal Existence

In some other universe
we never existed.

our nuclei's never
sparked
or burnt in cataclysm

does that make you
as happy as
it makes me.

The Darkest Hours

All Consuming

The regret it is
all consuming; feeding on
my maybes and
stuttered untils,

and it will go on
and on
until there is nothing
left of me but
bitterness.

because
until you can accept the part
that you played,

the maybes
will keep on playing
their vinyl's

and the certains
will grow old
with dust.

The Darkest Hours

The Boys Will Be Boys?

If you can stand there
and lecture me on
the differences

that it wasn't
a violation.
just a silly little
game

the fun

the things that boys get up to
in the dark
and the things that they are
entitled to,

then you were
sober enough
to understand that

I said no

The Darkest Hours

My Ignorance Was Our Bliss

I miss the ignorance
that made us blissful.
it was easy then,

to smile,
put on a show
and pretend
to our little world
that all was ok

I truly thought it was.

I cannot do that anymore.

The Darkest Hours

Delicate Fractures

Things cracked
over our years

skulls and
souls

and finally
the relationship

that was never really
there
but wished it was

it was all a pretence;
that our delicate china
couldn't crack.

and that was the downfall

when the people we loved
realised the fractures

The Darkest Hours

that glue
couldn't put back
together

The Darkest Hours

The Fault

It wasn't your fault
that you couldn't
love me

but it wasn't
my fault either
for leaving you
when someone better
came along.

someone
who was capable of the things
you weren't

The Darkest Hours

The First Heartbreak

The first heartbreak
should've been
love

a boy

who sat with my best friend
at lunch
instead of me

a daylight crush
who couldn't love me
back

or the fuckboys
the ones that mothers
warn you about

the ones who we all pretended
had good intentions.

The Darkest Hours

not you

you were supposed
to love me forever

The Darkest Hours

Disconnected Calls

You left me a long,
long time before
I left you

In truth
you were never really
here

but by the time
our finale made it to curtain
it was you,
who blocked me

bolted doors,
disconnected phone lines,
and still told them

it's me
not you
who doesn't dial the call

The Darkest Hours

but there was never
a choice for me at all.

The Darkest Hours

Mirrored

You pointed out my flaws
whilst festering in
your own ugliness

you weren't unattractive
per say
but it was never
your looks that made us
walk away

The Darkest Hours

In The Existence of Dreams

In my wildest
and deepest fantasies
we are still together
happily

and even if only
in the existence of dreams
it is enough to carry me
onwards

The Darkest Hours

Exploding Hearts

It wasn't me ignoring you
I just couldn't take you in

If I had
my heart would have
exploded
and you would discover
the things that no one
was meant to know

The Darkest Hours

The Innocence of Time

I wished to grow,
a delicate flower;
because time was cruel

eating away at the happiness
and
the childhood ignorance
innocence stole from me.

cold and
calculating
with too much time
to fill that
it eats away and
feeds on souls

the dementors of
very beings

and I wished to be bigger
to have a chance at least

The Darkest Hours

of escape.

The Darkest Hours

In The Past

When we said
it was all in
our past

I knew
you were lying

and now back
in the present
with our best intentions
laid bare
and true

fate has brought us
back here
once more

to the hill
where we'll say
it's all in the past.

The Darkest Hours

Young And Beautiful

I would wonder if
you would still love me
when I wasn't
young and
beautiful

and now I know
that it was silly

you never loved me then
either.

The Darkest Hours

The Devil's Eyes

My father's eyes pierced me
and now
my children too

because
I have
my father's eyes

The Darkest Hours

If The Looks Could Kill

You looked at me
in so many ways

but not ever in the way
you should have

as property,
a possession
like meat at
the cattle market

not like
I was your child.

The Darkest Hours

Comfort

It wasn't comforting
to know that you
never loved me

it was heart-breaking

The Darkest Hours

Good Enough

Now that I will
say goodbye
I want you to know
I am sorry

I tried
in ways that stabbed
my soul
I really did try

but it was never
good enough

I was never
good enough

The Darkest Hours

Sandcastles

Waves crash the sand
destroying childish castles,
that are now
broken homes

I liked them that way

it made me feel
less alone

The Darkest Hours

The Illusion of Word Play

It was all
an illusion,
that I was ok

a magic act

I wasn't

everything slowly dimmed
like candles eating us for supper;
necrotising smiles
into frowns

of pain
and feeling down

but I would die
before I told you

because it would
kill you to hear those words
escape from my mouth.

The Darkest Hours

You Shouldn't Be Here

I am holding on
with a silent grasp
to something

and it's something
that shouldn't exist
but painfully does

The Darkest Hours

The Darkest Hours

the end

The Darkest Hours

The Lakes

I see you on the lake,
shipwrecked without a compass.
my arms can't reach you
and I know it's pointless trying.

But I'll never stop.

I know I can't save you.

The Darkest Hours

Grief

the thing about grief is
it isn't about death.
at a guess it's about love
and all that comes with her

and it kills me inside out
to know
that I will never love someone
the way I loved
you

maybe that
is a good thing

because loving you
destroyed me
and now I am infested
with grief

but now
that we have met our end

The Darkest Hours

and said our final goodbye
one way
or another
I realise

the thing about grief is
it isn't always sad.
I don't miss your empty goodbyes.

the scars will heal
and the smiles will return,
long before you are dead
and that is how
we will end.

The Darkest Hours

Love

it's not the words
and the endless threats
that ends us.

the pills
or the rope
that binds us with death.

it's the lack of love
that catches up with us
in the end,
 and this note
I am writing is
the final curtain.

The Darkest Hours

Moonlit Sonatas

a song once played
in a house I used to know.
its notes danced along corridors of
power and unjust cruelty.

a girl sits alone
at the piano she will never own
teardrops playing
her final sonata.

the song plays again now
in the house I own.
its melody turned sorrows into
joy
centred around a mother
and her little boy.

The Darkest Hours

The Turning of Tables

one day
when the sky is bright
and the floods are
all washed away
we will meet,
once more.

four brown abysses
will interlock with
anguish
and shock.

i'll smile
and you'll frown and
bow your head
down to the ground
the shame tearing
into your flesh
it feels like dying.

and how the tables will turn.

The Darkest Hours

Interstellar

I stare out of a window of
some residence in London.

I let myself dream of you
that one day
you will return and save
this little girl engrossed in
the agonising guilt
about her decision
to walk away.

then I open my eyes
and the tears start
to flow.
it's foolish of me
to believe that
I am in your thoughts.
I left such a long time ago

but with the sound of chasing cars
I look up to the stars,

The Darkest Hours

knowing we stare up
at the same abyss.
and I am comforted that
by gazing at this sight

our eyes might
one day
meet again.

on a clear and
starless night

The Darkest Hours

Teardrops

I hear him awaken
rustling bedsheets shimming
a winding staircase
to paradise.

I wipe the tears
and hide the lies
my teardrops run tributaries
through a blonde abyss.

eyes peeled open
penetrating my soul
with blissful ignorance
innocently beautiful.

it's complicated
like unanticipated rain
but my beautiful boy
you'll never have to understand
what it's like
to carry this pain.

The Darkest Hours

Three Hundred and Sixty-Five Days

three hundred and sixty-five days
since I left

I am fine

but three hundred and sixty-five tears
have fallen,
because I let my mind
wonder.
how much longer will it hurt
until your voice grows
numb.

maybe another three hundred
and sixty-five
another lap around the sun
maybe then
I'll finally give up hope
that you were my one.

The Darkest Hours

The Wondering

at some point
on this god forsaken journey,
we have to stop wondering
why these things happened.

we may never know
and that's ok

because knowledge
and the truth
aren't mutually exclusive.

The Darkest Hours

Love like ours were Wars

one day
you will have to accept
that whatever occurred
between us
was never love

but it should have been

in the end
what we were left with
was nothing more
or short
of abuse,
with a gripping narrative
structure.

a war never destined to be won

The Darkest Hours

Returning

truthfully
even if it was possible
to go back,
to return

I wouldn't want to.

I know
too many things now
and it would be
the death of me.

The Darkest Hours

Healing

gasoline,
a box of matches
and a large prayer mat.

all essentials in a box of
healing from a childhood
void of love.

The Darkest Hours

Strength

sometimes strength is
lifting up
a forty-five-kilo body

and dragging it away
from gallon of tears
and heartbreak

because being broken
wasn't a viable option
anymore.

The Darkest Hours

Admissions

you tell your friends
that I died
all those years ago.

because for you
it is easier than admitting to
all of the things
you did to me.

The Darkest Hours

The Reason it Rained

It rained
to hide the tears:
concealing weakness from
a rifle fuelled by your sins

the rain washed away
rivers of tears
carrying with them the pain
I could no longer
withstand.

it rained
so that flowers could
grow

and now petunias stand
on a graveyard of woe.

The Darkest Hours

Paradise

nobody will understand
why I left that day.

because you marketed it
as a paradise.

when in reality
it was a world
ripe with pain.

The Darkest Hours

Dust to Dust

in the end
we are all just dust
a collection of bones.

a fragment
of our former selves.

maybe when
my being vacates
to places unknown

and we are narrowed down
to dust
you might start seeing me
as an equal.

or maybe just as
a human being.

The Darkest Hours

Purest Sins

the abused and
the abuser
but don't be mistaken

we may share the
same blood
but we will never be
the same.

The Darkest Hours

Blood on your hands

someday it will all become
too much.

a pot will come to boil
and slowly your secrets will secrete;
burn holes in crumpled attempts
of love

there is blood on
your hands.

the shock will turn to anger
and the anger
to grief

stood in disbelief
you cannot believe
what you have done.

but I got out.

The Darkest Hours

a sigh of relief.

someone will die in that house
but it isn't going to be
me.

The Darkest Hours

Desperation

I look at our lives
dog eared photographs
developed from
the crime scene.

or smashed picture frames,
my love seeping through
somehow.

It was all for show
but I wish it hadn't been

and now I am desperately
trying to paint
a mosaic
with colours I will never own

The Darkest Hours

Knowledge

did you think I was happy
then?

and do you know that
I am happy now.

The Darkest Hours

The Things You'll Never Be

the man you weren't is
the woman
I am going to be

this is for us

The Darkest Hours

Some Goodbyes Aren't Forever

There is nothing else
to say
except goodbye

but this isn't it

there will never be
a goodbye
for us.

you will always be with me

because a part of you
will always live
inside of me.

a voice that will haunt me
forever

The Darkest Hours

The Things Unsaid

There are poems
and songs that
I will never write.

soliloquies and sonatas
that will never marry
ink to paper.

because it is time
to lay us to rest.

and some stories
are best left unsaid.

The Darkest Hours

What Ifs

The dress I wore
just for you
is shimmering now,
in the moonlight

this is the hill.

the place where you wrap your arms
around me
and tell me
like our time is running out
that I was loved

because
even if I was
loosing myself,
I still had you.

standing here now
I know that none of it
is real

The Darkest Hours

It was nice to know
but it was all a show

some *what if*
that I should have discarded
a long time ago

The Darkest Hours

Running Circles

I cannot do it anymore

keeping on
running in circles
and tying myself
in knots

trying to get
people like you
to care about
people like me.

The Darkest Hours

Count Your Losses

you lost someone
who would have given
their whole life
for you

and I lost someone
who couldn't give
a damn

so, it will always be your loss
and my gain.

The Darkest Hours

The History Books

The rules
by which we were bound,
were meant to be broken

no woman
who toed the line
ever made
the history books.

The Darkest Hours

Wouldn't, Shouldn't, Couldn't

It hurts

the moving on.

watching the others laugh
about the things
we should have done

letting him put
his arms around my waist:
the security that
we will never have.

and loving
the children who came along
in the ways you couldn't
love me.

The Darkest Hours

Realisations

I realise
I was just nothing
to you

but for me
you were everything

and sure
I can erase you from this life
but not from my memories

you are everywhere

my soul
my mind
the air that I breathe
that right now is suffocating
me

slowly but surely

I am dying

The Darkest Hours

and now again,
I notice how

we are back to being
strangers
once more

The Darkest Hours

The Missing Piece

We are all
so much more than
the stories our tears
have written,

of joy
and sorrows
chosen like magpies.

the burdens we carry
in the scars
that we cover

and the hearts we conceal
with mole holed shirt sleeves.

we are complex creatures
unsolved
like puzzles,

until our one

The Darkest Hours

comes along
with the piece
we have been missing
all of this time.

The Darkest Hours

Fatal Disguises

I would still
die for you.

and I sat with that pain
for such a long time
until she told me that grief
is who she really was.

The Darkest Hours

I Can See You

I can see you
in the everywhere I go

the cracks in my walls;
sleeping dust
and centuries paint spilling out
and
into the bloodstream

in the passers by
who pretend to care and
stab your ageing bruise,
as our dust splatters
into the air

and in the wounds
I try so desperately
to hide

I see you
and maybe,

The Darkest Hours

in another time,
it won't make me cry.

The Darkest Hours

The Prospect of Living

This time last year
the itinerary looked
so very different.

the prospect of living
unbelievable

and the thought of us
happy together
unimaginable

and here I am
despite it all
on the X Day as we
fashionably called it

hoping that
if there is another lifetime

the next time we speak
 the prospects will be greater

The Darkest Hours

Stages Of Life

At every stage
of my life

I start to forgive you
a little less

for what you did
to me

The Darkest Hours

Our Story

Things had to change
the minute I had realised
your truth

I am ending
your chapter
because stories need more
than just villains
and heartbreak.

The Darkest Hours

Cutting The Wire

I gave you so many chances
too many

and you didn't listen

no easy decision
but now I must
cut our wires
and watch you fall

The Darkest Hours

Time

Time heals you
maybe not now
or tomorrow
even soon

so that one day
you will come back
to this place
and it will all be
so very different.

the same moon
and the same stars
but a different kind of love

one that doesn't leave scars.

The Darkest Hours

No Strings Attached

His love wasn't meant
for you

If it was
it would have come with
no strings attached.

The Darkest Hours

The Changing of The Tide

I know that
I cannot change your past
or our present

but I will change
my future
because we all
deserved better.

The Darkest Hours

The Loved

I loved you enough
to stay with you

but
love myself enough now
to walk away from you.

The Darkest Hours

The Pretence

You must ask yourself
the unimaginable.

was it really love,
or someone just playing
the cruel game of pretence?

The Darkest Hours

The Old Souls Home

This house is
an old folk's home
for young souls

the ones that grew up
too fast

and came
before their time

this place is for us
their time is here
and now.

The Darkest Hours

The Thoughts of Worth

I sometimes wonder
whether it was
worth it

to have and to hold
and to stay so long
with you

for you.

I don't think it was

The Darkest Hours

When We Were Young

When we were six
the cobblestones grew
the foundations laid out,
making way for the
painful new

and by the time
we were eight
glasses shattered
crushed under foot
like childish fantasies

eyes blackened
but hope bright
and children's books
collecting soot by night.

but when we were ten
we thought it would be
over by then
but we couldn't have been
closer to wrong

The Darkest Hours

night after night
our circumstances slipped further
from right

our only lullabies
a birdsong

and for years I wrote

of a light
at the end of
our darkest hours

and fickle beliefs
like the wildest dreams
we were never
permitted
to imagine

it came so soon
but all too late
because by that time
the childhood had gone,
out of date.

The Darkest Hours

each day growing sour
more and more
with every hour

The Darkest Hours

This Love

The love was unconditional
and unrequited

until it ended

when I stopped loving
a man
who could never
love me back.

The Darkest Hours

A Silent Stillness

The stillness
it shows
that there is nothing
between us
anymore

but air

so I think that it's time
for me
to go

The Darkest Hours

Continental Drift

With boundaries mapped out
like continents
I'll drift away
and leave you
behind

sailing towards a new
because when they see me

they see you

and it hurts so much,
I cannot breathe
the grief sucking the air
from us
before it hits

The Darkest Hours

A Letter from The One Who Got Out

my heart has split open,
spilling out onto a page.
glossed paper.
no expense spared.

I do not know what it is
I would like to say to you.
I have dreamt,
almost drooled at the thought of
this moment.

the how's and the
why's and the
fuck yous.

but now staring at the starting line,
the race now in front of us,
I seem a little lost for words.

Like I was all those years ago.
I guess what I wanted to say is,
we are doing ok,

The Darkest Hours

on our own.

I thought that losing you would be the
death of me,
but it turns out it was just you.

you were slowly killing me.

we would fight.
we would kiss,
and then we would make up.
every time,
over and over again.

it was worthless.
because nothing changed.

our love was toxic.
you were dynamite
and I was a hand grenade.

it was never going to work,
because I kept trying to love you
and you kept pointing the finger,
of blame.

The Darkest Hours

I know you do not care
and maybe it's better this way
a whole damn sight easier to bear.

for both of us.

my dearest

I love you, still,
but I am doing ok without you.

The Darkest Hours

It Ends with Us

I'm ready to move on
no more fighting
or slamming doors.
I refuse to let anyone else
carry your shit.

this ends with us.

The Darkest Hours

Postscript

Hello
it's me

bareboned and
bloodshot
all opened up to you

bruises
the ones you gave me
aged like the fine wines you spilt
on our etched contracts
of love

and scars cascade
they are my poisoned vines

this is me
I promise
no tricks to be played

no bricks in fists
or foul play planned

The Darkest Hours

no more fighting
the war is over

this is us
saying goodbye
to all the pain,
and the everything
we couldn't be

and me
still missing you
with the only piece of heart
I have left

a postscript
written by me and
just for you.

The Darkest Hours

about the author

Chloé Marcellino is an actor, poet and author, best known for her debut work, *The Darkest Hours,* in 2023. Chloé explores her experiences from her own childhood, encompassing this with the experiences of others, expressing this in a poetic symphony
that melts hearts and makes tears flow. She moved to London in 2022 and reads law at university.

Printed in Great Britain
by Amazon